AMBULANCE

A290 UOU

© 1988 Franklin Watts

Franklin Watts
12a Golden Square
London W1

Franklin Watts Australia
14 Mars Road
Lane Cove
N.S.W. 2066

ISBN: 0 86313 715 6

Design: Edward Kinsey

Typesetting: Lineage, Watford
Printed in Italy
by G. Canale & C. S.p.A. Turin

The Publishers, author and photographer
would like to thank the Avon and Somerset
Police for their help and co-operation. They
are especially grateful to Sergeant Steve
Scott and his colleagues at the Bristol
Traffic Unit who helped in the preparation
of this book, and to Debbie Pugh-Jones for
her invaluable assistance. The photographs
of traffic offenders were specially created
for the purposes of this book and do not
show actual law breakers or offences.

Police motorcyclist

Tim Wood
Photographs: Chris Fairclough

Franklin Watts
London/New York/Sydney/Toronto

I am a motor cycle
police officer.

I plan the day's work in my office.

I brief the other motor cycle officers.

I get my motor cycle ready.

I check all the equipment in my saddlebags.

I fill the petrol tank.

I check the tyre pressures.

I put on my leather coat and safety armbands.

I put on my heated gloves
and crash helmet.

My motor cycle can move quickly through heavy traffic.

I listen to the police radio
in my helmet.

I get off my motor cycle to direct traffic.

I stop a lorry
to check its load.

I escort an ambulance
to the hospital.

I escort a judge to the law courts.

I help a driver
whose car will not start.

I book a driver
who has broken the law.

I help a driver who is lost.

I write a ticket for a driver
parked on double yellow lines.

25

I return my bike to the garage
at the end of the day.

FACTS ABOUT MOTOR CYCLE POLICE OFFICERS

Motorcycle police officers go through a long period of training. They work for at least a year as police car drivers. Then they take several motor cycle riding courses lasting over 18 months in total.

Motor cycle police officers are usually over 30 years of age.

Motor cycle police officers can go faster than the speed limit if they have to. They can go through red traffic lights as long as they give way to the traffic.

The motor cycle shown in this book is a Norton Interpol 2. It can travel at over 200kph.

The saddlebags hold: First Aid kit, truncheon, handcuffs, maps, fire extinguisher, wet weather clothing, a red/green lamp and a book of traffic law.

A police radio is connected to speakers in the motor cycle police officer's helmet. He operates it with his knee using a long switch.

GLOSSARY

Book
To report someone who has broken the law.

Briefing
Telling police officers what their duties will be for the day.

Handcuffs
Two metal bracelets joined by a chain which are locked around the wrists of someone who has broken the law.

Judge
A person who tries accused people in a law court.

Law court
A building where people who have broken the law go for trial.

Saddlebags
Boxes fixed to the motor cycle for holding equipment.

Ticket
An official form used for reporting someone who has broken the law.

Truncheon
A short club carried by police officers.

Tyre pressure
The amount of air in the tyres.

INDEX